The Poetry of Dora Sigerson Shorter

VOLUME VI – UNCOLLECTED

Dora Mary Sigerson was born in Dublin on August 16th, 1866, the daughter of George Sigerson, a surgeon and writer, and Hester (née Varian) also a writer.

Her father was a leader in Dublin's intellectual world and immersed the young Dora in the vibrant literary society of Dublin throughout her childhood, helping her gain a deep and complete love of her country. Like her father, Dora was active in the Irish literary revival, and a passionate campaigner for home rule.

Her poetry collections date from 1893 and are particularly evocative when she writes of her homeland, War and, most of all, the Easter Rising of 1916. Her friends included Katharine Tynan, the noted Irish poet and author as well as fellow writers and poets Rose Kavanagh and Alice Furlong

When she married Clement King Shorter, an English journalist and literary critic, in 1895 they moved to England and she wrote under the name Dora Sigerson Shorter. Although in England her heart's passion remained with Ireland.

The tragic events of Easter 1916, were a terrible blow to her and her health quickly began to fail.

Dora Mary Sigerson Shorter died on January 6th, 1918. The cause of her death was not disclosed.

As well as a foremost poet Dora's talents extended to sculpture, journalism and novels.

Dora's best-known sculpture is the memorial in Glasnevin Cemetery to the executed leaders of the Easter Rebellion.

In her lifetime she was renowned for her personal beauty and her charm. That charm is reflected in her works which are full of eagerness, love, sympathy, and, of course, suffering.

Index of Contents

DORA SIGERSON - A TRIBUTE AND SOME MEMORIES by Katharine Tynan

To think of Dora Sigerson—and it is a poignant thought—takes one back to Dublin in the 'nineties, or the later 'eighties. I think it was on a summer Sunday in 1887 that Dr. Sigerson came to see me with his two daughters and Rose Kavanagh, whom I already knew. The Yeatses were there that Sunday for the big meal at a most unfashionable hour, which was a feature of those years for the young writers and artists of Dublin. My old home was in the country, just under the Dublin mountains, and, I think, a very delightful place.

Everyone, of course, knew Dr. Sigerson by repute. The house was full of the young that day, with just a sprinkling of the young of heart like Mr. Yeats and my father and Dr. Sigerson. I remember that my brother said to me, "Miss Sigerson is very beautiful." She was. Her face then had some curious suggestion of the Greek Hermes. She wore her dark hair short, and it was in heavy masses. She had a beautiful brow and eyebrows, very fine grey eyes, a short straight nose, a warm pale colour, and vivid red lips. A little later the Irish-American, Miss Louise Imogen Guiney, dedicated her "Roadside Harp" to the Sigerson sisters:

There in the Druid brake,
If the cuckoo be awake
Again, oh, take my rhyme,
And keep it long for the sake
Of a bygone primrose-time.
You of the star-bright head
That twilight thoughts sequester:
You to your native fountains led,
Like to a young Muse garlanded:
Dora, and Hester.

Dora was indeed "like to a young Muse garlanded." She was singularly beautiful, with some strange hint of storm in her young beauty. She was so full of artistic impulse and achievement of many kinds, and she arrived at so much of art without any apprenticeship that the word "genius" seems not inapplicable to her. Our friendship flowed straight on from that summer Sunday of 1887. Dr. Sigerson's house in Clare Street became my headquarters when I went into Dublin from my country home. Dora was always painting or writing or doing sculpture. I can remember her coming from somewhere downstairs to the drawing-room at No. 3, Clare Street, when I was announced, wearing a sort of sculptor's blouse. There is still in her old home, crowded with beautiful things, at least one head by her of a nymph or a dryad, strangely delicate and pensive.

I don't think she had read much poetry till John O'Leary, saying her poetry was too introspective, gave her Percy's "Reliques," whence the genesis of her fine ballad poetry. If she had any training as an art student for her painting and drawing and sculpture, it must have been very slight. The gifts came to her out of the air, so to speak; real gifts and nothing acquired.

For seven good years my life was inextricably interwoven with hers and Hester's. We had the same friends, the same merry-makings, the same tastes and aims. We were of the circle which revolved around the great old Fenian, John O'Leary, and his not less noble sister; we visited the American poets, Mr. and Mrs. Piatt, at Queenstown, where Mr. Piatt was American Consul; we spent many happy days at Mr. Richard Ashe King's delightful house at Waltham Terrace, Blackrock. We wrote for the same papers. Presently Dora Sigerson and I were together in politics, both Parnellites when the "split" came. Together we attended Mr. Parnell's meetings; we went to meet him when he returned to Dublin from the country; we lived through all the passionate loyalty of those days. Together we exulted; together we mourned; together we followed our chief to the grave, not thinking upon how she should one day lie near him.

Perhaps the best holiday we had together was a scamper through Donegal on some business about the industries for Lady Aberdeen. It was just before I was married. From the time we left Amiens Street Station till we returned it was all pure enjoyment. The people with their beautiful manners, the wonderful scenery, the hotels, the car-drivers, the priests, the little towns, the wild, lonely places, the great hospitality—all were a delight to her. She was full of the joie de vivre, despite the hint of tragedy in her beauty. She did madcap things. Like Martin Ross she could mimic animals perfectly. How we laughed when she crowed like a cock over a low wall beyond which was a poultry-yard, and the real Vizier, after one careful look around, marshalled all his ladies into an inner enclosure. I have somewhere a book of that tour with her delightfully humorous drawings. She was always pencil in hand. We did the whole of Donegal within a fortnight, and came back, blowzed but happy, I to my wedding, she to the

Dublin she always loved. A year or two later she met Clement Shorter at our little house in Mount Avenue, Ealing.

One thing I must not omit to mention—her passionate love of animals. In the old, good days in Dublin she used to pick up waifs and strays of forlorn doghood and take them to the Dogs' Home. The boys in the street used to shout derision at us: "Go on! wid yer grand hats and ye to be starvin' yer dog!" The sense of humour supported us.

How we laughed and lived together! Ah, well:

Let nothing disturb thee,
Let nothing affright thee.
All passes,
Only God remaineth
For ever and ever.

I will not speak of her beautiful poetry, essential poetry, always with a passionate emotion to give it wings. It is for the critic. No one will say she was not happy in her English life, though her heart was always slipping away like a grey bird to Ireland. She had a very full life and she had absolute devotion and knew what a precious thing she had.

Her breakdown in health was sudden. She attributed it herself to her intense and isolated suffering—isolated beyond the perfect sympathy of her devoted husband—over the events following Easter week, 1916, in Dublin, and the troubles which menaced the country she adored. I think she need not have felt so bitterly isolated; the spirit of humanity is strong in the good English—and the good English are very good—but the fact remains that she broke her heart over it all; and so she died, as she would have chosen to die, for love of the Dark Rosaleen.

DORA SIGERSON by C. P. Curran

The finest side of Irish life and literature is poorer to-day by the death of Dora Sigerson. From her long residence in England she was known here mainly as a poet of a genius as distinguished as it was personal. But when, in recent years, affairs in Ireland grew more critical, her great-hearted personality emerged more clearly and shone the more brightly as the situation grew more dangerous. Love of Ireland was with her a passion. The events of Easter week moved her profoundly. She spent herself regally on behalf of her people with brain, pen and fortune and at the expense of her vitality. The best of the English weeklies said that "the rebellion killed her almost as surely as if she had stood with the rebels in O'Connell Street. Henceforth she could think of little else; of what had died with it and what might live." That is no less than the truth. She is fairly to be reckoned with the dead of Easter. Devotion to their cause consumed her like a flame into which she flung all her gifts, neither few nor negligible. She was a true artist, eagerly seeking expression for an ardent and manifold personality which itself transcended all her work, whether in poetry, sculpture or painting. Her poetry was saluted by the greatest contemporary names in England: Meredith, Francis Thompson, Swinburne, and the present writer has seen her name as the subject of lecture on the noticeboards of the Sorbonne. What faults lay on the surface of her verse were more than compensated for by its intensity, an intensity often tragic, "stoned by continual wreckage of her dreams," but always filled with pity. In the "Songs of the Irish

Rebellion" and in her later work generally which we, in Ireland, will always consider her best, the passion that consumed her burnt away these superficial defects, themselves characteristic of her impetuous spirit. The poet of "Ireland," of the "Wind on the Hills," of "Ceann Dubh Dilis," of "Sixteen Dead Men," will always be remembered on that honourable roll of artists who, to the gain of both, fused with their art, the strong love of the people.

THE DEAD WIFE

Thrice turned she in her narrow bed,
His tears disturbed her rest;
She kissed the little babe that lay
So still upon her breast.

"Dream well," she said, "my daughter dear,
Since I must leave you lone;
Three times your father's piteous voice
Did make a grievous moan;

"Three times your father's bitter cry
Did wake me from my sleep,
So must I go and comfort him
And bid him not to weep."

Her fingers chill she did unlace
From off her breast so white;
"Poor hands," quoth she, "oft for his sake
You toiled a weary night"

She stepped out from her grave so green
Upon her feet so slim,
"Oft were you wounded on the road
Where you did follow him."

Lone went she up the long boreen
Wherein her love did dwell.
And there she met a nut-brown maid
She once did love full well.

"Now God between us and all harm!"
The maid she fearful cried;
"I thought you slept within your grave,
Your little babe beside.

"I thought you lay all glad in rest
Who now doth walk alone;
What grief is on your soul, poor ghost,

What wrong would you atone?"

"My many sins I do deplore,"
The pale young ghost replied;
"Yet would I sleep to-night full well
My little babe beside.

"From Life's long road all weary I
Would hold such sleeping blest,
Save for the grief of one who mourns
And will not let me rest—

"Save for the tears of one I loved
O'er all the world beside,
Who held me close unto his breast
And named me once his bride.

"I know, as no birds sing for me.
He dreads the thrushes' song;
Since I am lying in the dark.
He thinks the day too long.

"And so I left my little babe
All lone in her cold bed,
So I might draw him to my side
And dry the tears he shed;

"So I might bid him weep no more,
But Heaven's pity take,
That bade me forth to bring my dear
From grief and lone heartbreak;

"Within the shadow of the tomb
In one embrace to rest.
My shoulder for his weary head.
His babe upon my breast"

Now when the maiden all so pale
This piteous tale did hear,
She loosed her braids of nut-brown hair,
And dropped full oft a tear.

"Now go you back, poor ghost," said she,
"And may your sleep be sound;
And grieve you naught for any man
Who walks the upper ground.

"And do not wake for any soul

Who on this earth doth live;
For if your dear doth grieve him sore
You could not comfort give.

"For he doth weep the lone night through
And all the weary day.
Since I unto his suit am cold
And to his love say nay!"

THE DEER-STONE

A LEGEND OF GLENDALOUGH

It was the bride of Colman Dhu
In Glendalough sat down,
She hushed the babe upon her breast
Beside the lake so brown.

The mountains steep about her rose
All glad in green and gold.
The heart of all the waters deep
Again their glory hold.

Now had the bride of Colman Dhu
Looked long towards the west,
She there had seen the glowing sun
Slip slow towards his rest

But had she looked towards the east,
A maid there was to see.
Who bore two daggers in her eyes—
Black hate and jealousy.

She did not look towards the east,
Nor looked she to the south,
But closed her two white lids in sleep,
A smile on her red mouth.

Oh, had she seen the evil maid
Who death so stealthy bore,
She had not closed her lashes long
She now would raise no more.

Slow crept the witch unto her side,
Aiid saw with furious eye
The smiling two in slumber deep,

Who did so helpless lie.

"And for the tears, O Colman proud,
That I have shed for you,
Pll drive a sorrow in your breast
To break your heart in two.

"And for the words that you have said,
To crush me with disdain,
m hush the laughter on your lips
That shall not smile again."

Within her hand a deadly draught
She raised a moment up,
"And shall it be your little son
Who first must taste the cup?"

"Ah, no! For should your bride awake,
Her grief would mend your moan.
For you in pity at her tears
Would half forget your own.

"But if death lies upon her heart.
The two are surely slain;
The little babe must thirst and die,
And you are mine again."

She looked upon each lovely face
That held a soul asleep,
"And one shall drink of deadly wine,
A draught both long and deep."

She looked upon the baby lips
That curling 'neath her eyes,
Sought some sweet fountain in his dreams,
Ana fed with gentle sighs.

Then with a frown and muttered groan
Quick to the other crept,
And raised the cup in her false hand,
To slay them while they slept.

Ah, gentle Nature, at the deed
You quenched within the west
Your golden lamp, so none might see
The murder stand confessed.

Then thrice upon the frightened air,

The dying lips drew breath,
Twice in they drew the wine of life,
And once the draught of death.

Now Colman, with his spear in hand,
Late coming from the chase,
Heard the low weeping of a child
Within a lonesome place.

"Oh, hard your mother's heart," he said,
"Your cries she will not hear!"
Quick from his steed he sprang, and saw
His wife and child so dear.

Soft came the weeping of the babe
Whose fount had grown so cold.
He flung himself upon the earth,
And did his wife enfold.

All silent was she to his cries,
Her cheek was cold as death,
And to his hot impassioned kiss
Came no responsive breath.

And when he saw that she was dead
He rose up to his feet.
And wrapped her in his hunting coat
To make her winding sheet.

"Mo Chree," he said, "your bed to-night
Will be both dark and cold,
On what new island will you wake,
Or what strange face behold?

"Asthór," he said, "lest you should fear
To wander forth alone,
I'll follow through the gates of death
To claim you for my own."

Into his fond and loving heart
He drove his hunting knife,
And by his bride's chill side he lay,
And soon gave up his life.

It was the good St. Kevin went.
All bowed and lost in prayer,
And as he paced his lonely path
The young witch met him there.

And in her gown the poison cup
She did most quickly hide.
But spoke the good saint unto her,
And would not be denied.

"What evil thing is this?" he said,
"That you must put away?
It is no gracious act indeed
That fears the light of day."

"It is but bread," the witch replied,
"From my small store I take.
To feed a poor deserted babe,
I go for pity sake."

"Now, be it bread," the priest replied,
"I pray it multiply;
But if it is an evil thing,
Full heavy may it lie."

And then the priest, all deep in prayer,
Went forth his lonely way,
While stood the witch upon the path
In wild and deep dismay.

For in her robe the poison cup
Did all so heavy grow,
She scarce could stand upon her feet,
And could but slowly go.

Now when she reached the rugged rock
That held her hidden home,
The waters threw their magic up
And blinded her with foam.

She gave a sharp and sudden cry
And fell within the lake,
And so may perish all who sin,
And evil vengeance take.

But good St Kevin, deep in prayer,
His holy way did go.
Soon came to him the sound of grief,
Soft cries of bitter woe.

There in a dark and lonesome place
A little babe he found,

And, close beside, a lovely pair
AU cold upon the ground.

"Movrone, Movrone," the good saint cried,
"What evil deed is here?"
And for their beauty and their youth
He shed a bitter tear.

He dug for them a lonely grave,
A grave both wide and deep.
"And slumber well," he softly said,
"Till God shall end your sleep."

He knelt him down upon his knee
Their lonely bed beside,
And then he saw the little babe
That weak in hunger cried.

He raised it up in his two hands.
And held it close and warm,
"O Christ," he said, "your mercy give
To keep this child from harm.

"Oh, pitiful indeed is this
Poor little one alone,
Whose dead lie peaceful in their sleep
While he doth make his moan.

"O Mary, who in Bethlehem
Held once upon thy breast
A tender babe, look down on this
Who is so sore oppressed.

"I have no food for this poor child.
Who must with hunger die.
Thy mercy give," the good priest prayed
With many a piteous sigh.

He looked across the waters deep,
And to the hills so brown.
And lo ! a shy wood creature there
All timidly came down.

And thrice it sprang towards the west.
And thrice towards the east.
It was as though some hand unseen
Drove forth the gentle beast.

But when the little child it heard,
That still with hunger cried.
It sprang before the guiding hand,
And stood the babe Inside.

And in a hollowed stone it shed
Its milk so warm and white,
And then, all timid, stood apart
To watch the babe's delight.

And at each eve and every mom
The gentle doe was there,
To find the little babe, and see
The saint, all deep in prayer.

In Glendalough the stone lies still
All plainly to be seen.
And many folk will point the place
Where once the milk had been.

THE DEAN OF SANTIAGO

The Dean of Santiago on his mule
Rode quick the Guadalquivir banks along,
He had no eye the veiling eve to love,
No ear to listen for the bird's late song.

Gold mist and purple of the setting sun,
Rose lapping wave and linnet's low good-night,
The crags that sat the hills like kings enthroned,
All heather-crowned, for him had no delight.

His roaming glances go from east to west,
Climb quick before him, find amid the rocks
A hut; he hastens, casting free his mule,
And with no gentle hand the door he knocks.

"Now who would enter?" "I, the Dean, let pass."
He sees the tenant working at his books,
"And what can I, a student, poor, remote,
Do for the Dean?" he answers to his looks.

"Teach me your magic, so I learn to slave
The hiding creatures from the circling air
And bid them speak. Blow from the crystal globe
The mists that hold my future clouded there."

"What? Share my magic! But it were not well:
The Church such study doth denounce and shun."
The Dean with some rebuke now makes reply,
"My law I own in this—let it be done."

"Then you must eat before the task is set:
Well, when you finish; since you eager are
We should begin. Nay, this I do insist.
For you are weary, having travelled far.

"Hussein!"—he bids the servant by his side—
"Go tell the cook a guest with me will dine;
And let two capons be prepared by him,
And two gold cups of my most famous wine.

"Tie up the straying mule. And now begone;
The Dean within an hour will dine with me."
The servant goes, and lets the curtain fall,
And darkness folds the room in mystery.

Soft wings brush past the Dean, strange sounds Boat up,
Like tongues that have no words, through the still air.
"What say you?" leans the Dean with eager ears
And grasping hands that find no substance there.

"What are you?" But the magic mist is gone,
Hussein has entered, and the light let through.
"A message for the Dean." He reads in haste,
"The Bishop being dead, we send for you."

The Dean arises full of pompous pride :
"If I am Bishop, I shall not forget
My student-teacher, and shall bid you come
To teach that lore I leave with much regret."

A month has passed—the Bishop in his room
Receives the student bowing at his feet.
With some delight, and says he has prepared
A secret chamber where they can repeat

Their former study, and so follow it.
The student, smiling gratitude, doth speak,
"I beg a boon of you," and hears reply,
"I make a promise, and I never break.

"The boon is yours." The student bows again:
"I have a son, a gentle youth and good,

Who seeks the Church." The Bishop lifts his eyes,
"To him I hold the hand of brotherhood.

"Soon I shall call him, but to-day my time
Is thick with thought, because a rumour came
The great Archbishop at the door of Death
Doth knock—the air is heavy with my name."

A year goes by, and the Archbishop wakes,
Springs from his bed, and "Hussein, you!" he cries,
To find strange eyes upon him. Bows the Moor,
"My master waits your message," he replies.

"Then bid him enter, take up his abode
Within my Palace, wait until I come.
To-day my mind is busy with such things
That bid me to all other thoughts be dumb.

"Go, tell your master, he will understand.
The Cardinal is dying. What I His son
Begs for a hope I What better hope than this—
The Cardinal is dying?—I have done."

The Cardinal upon his throne reclines,
And at his feet the student, bowing low,
"A boon, my lord, a boon—let me begone.
Back to my solitude I fain would go.

"Here comes the world between me and my art,
My soul is weary and my body ill,
My study broken, and my time misspent;
You have forgotten what was once your will."

"Nay, friend," the other cries, "you are unjust;
My heart is with you, and I pray you stay
Until my mind breaks from the bonds of care
That hold it now—a little more delay.

"Have you not heard the rumour that goes forth—
The Pope is dying? Who shall fill his chair
When he has passed all sainted to the grave?
Peace, friend, until the occupant is there."

The Pope within his chamber, deep in thought.
Hears at his door a knock, and saying, "Come,"
The student bends before him with reproach,
"From all my knowledge you have picked no crumb.

"O Holiness! we had no feast of lore.
But fortune came to you beneath my star.
Then let me go, since me you do not wish,
Now you are greater than all others are."

"Old man," the Pope replied," I let you go
In pity of your age and fading hair,
Whom I should prison in my dungeon deep
For all the evil magic you did dare

"Reveal to me, who only sought your side
To find your wickedness and give it light
Go back into your wilderness, but leave
Your ways of darkness. Get you from my sight."

"O Holiness," the student bent and said,
"My son for whom you promised of your aid";
"Begone!" the Pope replied; "think not I should
By son of you the Christian Church degrade."

"I go, great Holiness, without a fee
For all my time ; now but one boon I hold;
To break my fast, I hunger as I go—
Give me one meal, the way is long and cold."

Now spake the Pope in anger, struck the bell,
"I call my guards to put this beggar out."
The door swings open, Hussein enters quick,
"What, you again?"—he rises in his doubt.

He gazes round, his Palace slips away,
A shadow-palace floating from his eyes.
"What ho! my guards," his voice falls into tears.
He rubs his lids to rid them of surprise.

"Hussein," the student smiles, "go tell the cook
One capon only, and one cup of wine,
And bring this ingrate's mule beside the door—
The Dean of Santiago will not dine."

THE DESERTED LOVER

I go through wet spring woods alone,
Through sweet green woods with heart of stone,
My weary foot upon the grass
Falls heavy as I pass.

The cuckoo from the distance cries,
The lark a pilgrim in the skies;
But all the pleasant spring is drear.
I want you, dear!

I pass the summer meadows by,
The autumn poppies bloom and die;
I speak alone so bitterly
For no voice answers me.
"O lovers parting by the gate,
O robin singing to your mate,
Plead, plead you well, for she will hear,
'I love you, dear!'"

I crouch alone, unsatisfied,
Mourning by winter's fireside.
Fate, what evil wind you blow.
Must this be so?
No Southern breezes come to bless,
So conscious of their emptiness
My lonely arms I spread in woe,
I want you so.

THE ENEMIES

I could have sung as sweet as any lark
Who in unfettered skies doth find him blest,
And sings to leaning angels prayer and praise,
For in God's garden the most lowly nest.

But came the cares — a grey and stinging throng
Of liliputian foes, whose thrust and dart
Did blind my eyes and hush my song in tears;
Their brushing wings flung poison to my heart

I could have fought, in truth, a goodly fight,
Braved death, nor feared defeat before one foe;
Against these puny cares I strive in vain.
They sting my soul unto its overthrow.

THE ENCHANTED LAKE

I found a dark enchanted lake,
That lay within a lonely glade;

I stood a moment, held entranced.
Hid 'neath the willow's purple shade.

The moon cast down her silver nets,
As slow she sailed the misty blue,
And in their twisting coil and mesh
The leaping waters softly drew.

Like some young nun, vain in the night,
The white magnolia blossom bent
All timid down her face to view
Within that favoured element.

"Why from rough seas did Venus rise,
And wherefore let her beauty glow
From chill embraces of the wave.
If she this fairy spot did know?"

I thought: "From this enchanted lake,
That holds the heavens on its heart,
Should she have risen in the night
And flung the clinging waves apart."

Lo! as I spoke the purple shade
Rang out in some sweet elfin tune,
And singing 'neath my gaze, a nymph
Flashed in the pale net of the moon.

"Ye gods, look down," I knelt and cried:
"This scented pool is sure a cup
Lost from your board, upon whose lip
A precious pearl is offered up.

"Or if they sleep, O nymph, on me
Some pity take, and seek the shore,
Or draw me in your white embrace
Down to your home for evermore."

For one sweet moment did she stand,
A gleaming statue washed in tears;
Her snowy breast alone did tell
The tragic tumult of her fears.

Then, like some bird who feels a wound,
She gave her voice to little cries.
But ere she fluttered to the shade
She looked on me with Laura's eyes.

Ah! This white fairy of the lake,
Who by her magic did entrance,
Held one brief moment my poor heart,
All faithless, only by a glance.

To you, my Laura, ever true,
Who now pass by with much disdain,
And will not listen to my vows,
But let me plead, and plead in vain;

Who turn away with blushing cheek
And head averted at my sigh,
Whose scornful laughter chills my heart,
So that I pine, and soon must die.

Ah! who beside that sheltered lake
Did thus my secret love surprise?
I swear the nymph was nought to me,
Save that she looked with Laura's eyes.

THE FAIR LITTLE MAIDEN

"There is one at the door, Wolfe O'Driscoll,
At the door, who bids you to come!"
"Who is he that wakes me in the darkness,
Calling when all the world is dumb?"

"Six horses has he to his carriage.
Six horses blacker than the night.
And their twelve red eyes in the shadows—
Twelve lamps he carries for his light;

"His coach is a herse black and mouldy,
Within a coffin open wide:
He asks for your soul, Wolfe O'Driscoll,
Who doth call at the door outside."

"Who let him thro' the gates of my gardens,
Where stronger bolts have never been?"
"The father of the fair little maiden
You drove to her grave deep and green."

"And who let him pass through the courtyard.
Loosening the bar and the chain?"
"Who but the brother of the maiden
Who lies in the cold and the rain!"

"Then who drew the bolts at the portal.
And into my house bade him go?"
"The mother of the poor yoimg maiden
Who lies in her youth all so low."

"Who stands, that he dare not enter.
The door of my chamber, between?"
"O, the ghost of the fair little maiden
Who lies in the churchyard green."

THE FAIRIES

The fairies, the fairies, the mischief-loving fairies,
Have stolen my loved one, my darling, and my dear;
With charms and enchantments they lured and waylaid him,
So my love cannot comfort and my presence cannot cheer.

The fairies, the fairies, I'll love no more the fairies:
I'll never sweep the hearth for them or care the fairy thorn,
I'll skim no more the yellow cream nor leave the perfumed honey;
But I'll drive the goats for pasture to their greenest rath each morn.

With Ave, and Ave, and many a Paternoster,
Within their magic circle I'll tell my beads for you;
My prayers be sharp as arrows to pierce their soulless bosoms
Till they come with loud sorrow to tell me that they rue.

My darling, my darling, what glamour is upon you
That you find for your gaze satisfaction and content
In the charms of that colleen, with her black snaky ringlets,
Her red lips contemptuous, and her gloomy brows so bent?

The fairies, the fairies, from her blue eyes were peeping;
They blew her hair about you so you were lost, my dear.
With their charms and enchantments they lured and waylaid you,
So my love cannot comfort and my presence cannot cheer.

THE FAIRY THORN-TREE

"This is an evil night to go, my sister,
To the thorn-tree across the fairy rath,
Will you not wait till Hallow Eve is over?
For many are the dangers in your path!"

"I may not wait till Hallow Eve is over,
I shall be there before the night is fled.
For, brother, I am weary for my lover.
And I must see him once, alive or dead.

"I've prayed to heaven, but it would not listen,
I'll call thrice in the devil's name to-night,
Be it a live man that shall come to hear me.
Or but a corpse, all clad in snowy white."

She had drawn on her silken hose and garter.
Her crimson petticoat was kilted high.
She trod her way amid the bog and brambles,
Until the fairy-tree she stood near-by.

When first she cried the devil's name so loudly
She listened, but she heard no sound at all;
When twice she cried, she thought from out the darkness
She heard the echo of a light footfall.

When last she cried her voice came in a whisper,
She trembled in her loneliness and fright;
Before her stood a shrouded, mighty figure,
In sombre garments blacker than the night.

"And if you be my own true love," she questioned,
"I fear you! Speak you quickly unto me."
"O, I am not your own true love," it answered,
"He drifts without a grave upon the sea."

"If he be dead, then gladly will I follow
Down the black stairs of death into the grave."
"Your lover calls you for a place to rest him
From the eternal tossing of the wave."

"I'll make my love a bed both wide and hollow,
A grave wherein we both may ever sleep."
"What give you for his body fair and slender,
To draw it from the dangers of the deep!"

"I'll give you both my silver comb and earrings,
I'll give you all my little treasure store."
"I will but take what living thing comes forward,
The first to meet you, passing to your door."

"O may my little dog be first to meet me,
So loose my lover from your dreaded hold."

"What will you give me for the heart that loved you,
The heart that I hold chained and frozen cold!"

"My own betrothed ring I give you gladly,
My ring of pearls—and every one a tear!"
"I will but nave what other living creature
That second in your pathway shall appear."

"To buy this heart, to warm my love to living,
I pray my pony meet me on return."
"And now, for his young soul what will you give me,
His soul that night and day doth fret and burn!"

"You will not have my silver comb and earrings,
You will not have my ring of precious stone;
O, nothing have I left to promise to you.
But give my soul to buy him back bis own."

All woefully she wept, and stepping homeward,
Bemoaned aloud her dark and cruel fate;
"O, come," she cried, "my little dog to meet me,
And you, my horse, be browsing at the gate."

Right hastily she pushed by bush and bramble.
Chased by a fear that made her footsteps fleet,
And as she ran she met her little brother.
Then her old father coming her to meet.

"O brother, little brother," cried she, weeping,
"Well you said of fairy-tree beware.
For precious things are bought and sold ere midnight,
On Hallow Eve, by those who barter there."

She went alone into the little chapel.
And knelt before the holy Virgin's shrine,
She wept, "O Mother Mary, pray you for me.
To save those two most gentle souls of thine."

And as she prayed, behold the holy statue
Spoke to her, saying, "Little can I aid,
God's ways are just, and you have dared to question
His judgment on this soul; you bought—and paid.

"For that one soul, your father and your brother.
Your own immortal life you bartered; then.
Yet one chance is allowed—your sure repentance.
Give back his heart you made to live again."

"For these two souls—my father and my brother—
I give his heart back into death's cold land.
Never again to warm his dead, sweet body,
Or beat to madness underneath my hand."

"And for your soul—to save it from its sorrow,
You must drive back his soul into the night,
Back into righteous punishment and justice.
Or lose your chance of everlasting light."

"O, never shall I drive him back to anguish,
My soul shall suffer, letting his go free."
She rose, and weeping, left the little chapel.
Went forward blindly till she reached the sea.

She dug a grave within the surf and shingle,
A dark, cold bed, made very deep and wide.
She laid her down all stiff and stretched for burial,
Right in the pathway of the rising tide.

First tossed into her waiting arms the restless
Loud waves, a woman very grey and cold,
Within her bed she stood upright so quickly,
And loosed her fingers from the dead hands' hold.

The second who upon her heart had rested
From out the storm, a baby chill and stark,
With one long sob she drew it on her bosom.
Then thrust it out again into the dark.

The last who came so slow was her own lover;
She kissed his icy face on cheek and chin,
"O cold shall be your house to-night, beloved,
O cold the bed that we must sleep within.

"And heavy, heavy, on our lips so faithful
And on our hearts, shall lie our own roof-tree."
And as she spoke the bitter tears were falling
On his still face, all Salter than the sea.

"And oh," she said, "if for a little moment
You knew, my cold, dead love, that I was by.
That my soul goes into the utter darkness
When yours comes forth—and mine goes in to die."

And as she wept she kissed his frozen forehead,
Laid her warm lips upon his mouth so chill,
With no response—and then the waters flowing

Into their grave, grew heavy, deep, and still.

And so, 'tis said, if to that fairy thorn-tree
You dare to go, you see her ghost so lone,
She prays for love of her that you will aid her,
And give your soul to buy her back her own.

THE FETCH

"What makes you so late at the trysting?
What caused you so long to be?
For a weary time I have waited
From the hour you promised me."

"I would I were here by your side, love,
Full many an hour ago,
For a thing I passed on the roadway
All mournful and so slow."

"And what have you passed on the roadside
That kept you so long and late?"
"It. is weary the time behind me
Since I left my father's gate.

"As I hastened on in the gloaming
By the road to you to-night,
There I saw the corpse of a young maid
All clad in a shroud of white."

"And was she some comrade cherished.
Or was she a sister dead,
That you left thus your own beloved
Till the trysting-hour had fled?"

"Oh, I would that I could discover.
But never did see her face,
And I knew I must turn and follow
Till I came to her resting place."

"And did it go up by the town path,
Did it go down by the lake?
I know there are but the two churchyards
"Where a corpse its rest may take."

"They did not go up by the town path,
Nor stopped by the lake their feet,

They buried the corpse all silently
Where the four cross-roads do meet."

"And was it so strange a sight, then,
That you should go like a child,
Thus to leave me wait all forgotten—
By a passing sight beguiled?"

"'Twas my name that I heard them whisper,
Each mourner that passed by me;
And I had to follow their footsteps,
Though their faces I could not see."

"And right well I should like to know, now,
Who might be this fair young maid,
So come with me, my own true love,
If you be not afraid."

He did not go down by the lakeside,
He did not go by the town,
But carried her to the four cross-roads,
And he there did set her down.

"Now, I see no track of a foot here,
I see no mark of a spade.
And I know right well in this white road
That never a grave was made."

And he took her hand in his right hand
And led her to town away.
And there he questioned tne good old priest.
Did he bury a maid that day.

And he took her hand in his right hand,
Down to the church by the lake,
And there he questioned the pale young priest
If a maiden her life did take.

But neither had heard of a new grave
In all the parish around.
And no one could tell of a young maid
Thus put in unholy ground.

So he loosed her hand from his hand,
And turned on his heel away,
And, "I know now you are false," he said,
"From the lie you told to-day."

And she said, "Alas I what evil thing
Did to-night my senses take?"
She knelt her down by the water-side
And wept as her heart would break.

And she said, "Oh, what fairy sight then
Was it thus my grief to see?
I will sleep well 'neath the still water,
Since my love has turned from me."

And her love he went to the north land,
And far to the south went he,
And her distant voice he still could hear
Call weeping so bitterly.

And he could not rest in the daytime,
He could not sleep in the night.
So he hastened back to the old road.
With the trysting place in sight.

What first he heard was his own love's name,
And keening both loud and long.
What first he saw was his love's dear face.
At the head of a mourning throng.

And all white she was as the dead are.
And never a move made she,
But passed him by in her lone black pall.
Still sleeping so peacefully.

And all cold she was as the dead are,
And never a word she spake,
When they said, "Unholy is her grave
For she her life did take."

And silent she was as the dead are,
And never a cry she made,
When there came, more sad than the keening,
The ring of a digging spade.

No rest she had in the old town church.
No grave by the lake so sweet,
They buried her in unholy ground,
Where the four cross roads do meet.

THE FOOLISH OLD MAN

A miller's daughter, as I heard tell—
Sing heigh! but the maid was merry—
Was loved by her father's man full well,
His cheek was brown as a berry.

He made the grey mare fast to her stall,
The red cow drove to the byre,
Then he sought the old man in his hall,
Where he sat before the fire.

Quoth he, "Old man, I have served you true,
Full twenty years and over,
Now your daughter's hand I do beg from you
That she wed her faithful lover."

When the farmer heard the youth so speak
There was not reason in him,
His anger like a storm did break,
He feared he could not win him.

Cried he, "Rash youth, since you dare to nurse
This dream,—this secret wooing,
If you should wed, may a father's curse
Be your swift and sure undoing.

"My curse shall feed on your fields of corn,
On your roof-tree make its nesting,
Your wife shall wish your child unborn
As he pines on her sore heart resting."

Now when this cruel oath he said
The youth did chide him, crying,
"Since I have neither field nor bed
Your curse shall fall to dying.

"But if I had yon broad grass land,
And there put roof and rafter,
I vow revenge were to your hand
And you'd have all the laughter."

"If that be so," the old man cried,
Unto the faithful lover,
"Take you yon keep the wood beside,
And me land that it doth cover.

"So my oath fall on land and lot,
On house and home forever.

Your wife shall pine on the cursed spot,
I shall be beaten never!"

When thus he spoke in anger wild,
The youth did stay him, saying,
"Since I have neither wife nor child
Still goes your curse delaying.

"But should I win for my true bride
Some day your own fair daughter,
Alack I not then your will denied
To make a grievous slaughter."

When the old man this tale did hear.
He tried no more to stay him,
He gave the youth his daughter dear.
So that his curse might slay him.

All silent he for a year and a day
All lone with his rage and sorrow,
Then he spoke his wrath, "Too long I stay,
I will seek their roof to-morrow."

At dawn he sprang on his old grey mare
And to their gate went speeding.
Pale at the door stood his daughter fair,
Her beauty was all exceeding.

Hushed in her arms was her son so dear,
As though she feared to lose him—
She laid the babe with a smile and a tear
Upon her father's bosom.

"Now curse, if you will, our good roof-tree
And all that doth lie under,
But spare our child, so dear," quoth she,
"Or cleave my heart asunder."

He had no curse for her piteous cry.
But his long lone love confessing,
With dim eyes raised to the morning sky.
He gave—a father's blessing.

THE HEART OF A MAID

In the heart of a rose

Lies the heart of a maid;
If you be not afraid
You will wear it. Who knows?

In the pink of its bloom,
Lay your lips to her cheek;
Since a rose cannot speak,
And you gain the perfume.

If the dews on the leaf
Are the tears from her eyes;
If she withers and dies,
Why, you have the belief,

That a rose cannot speak.
Though the heart of a maid
In its bosom must fade.
And with fading must break.

THE HERITAGE

He on his man-child laid a soothing hand.
And hushed him into slumber, singing, "Sleep!
For thee the world was made and for thee planned.
With this thy heritage, why dost thou weep?

"For thee the mother bird on her soft nest
Doth turn her speckled eggs with patient care.
And lists until they move beneath her breast,
To break to music in the summer air.

"For thee the flower in the still night lifts up
Her tender buds the drooping dew to stay,
So that each mom she hath a brimming cup
Of perfumed wine to pledge the coming day.

"For thee the beast at thy young feet lets fall
His crimson life, that thou mayst live and grow;
To hold the earth and all things great and small—
For thee were made the tides to ebb and flow.

"For thee the wondrous earth, so hush thy cries"—
He laid his hand upon the tumbled curls—
"And God's high paradise"; he sought the skies.
And there despairing saw—unnumbered worlds.

THE BALLAD OF THE LITTLE BLACK HOUND

Who knocks at the Geraldine's door to-night
In the black storm and the rain?
With the thunder crash and the shrieking wind
Comes the moan of a creature's pain.

And once they knocked, yet never a stir
To show that the Geraldine knew;
And twice they knocked, yet never a bolt
The listening Geraldine drew.

And thrice they knocked ere he moved his chair,
And said, "Whoever it be,
I dare not open the door to-night
For a fear that has come to me."

Three times he rises from out his chair,
And three times he sits him down.
"Now what makes faint this heart of mine?"
He says with a growing frown.

"Now what has made me a coward to-night,
Who never knew fear before?
But I swear the hand of a little child
Keeps pulling me from the door."

The Geraldine rose from his chair at last
And opened the door full wide;
"Whoever is out in the storm," said he,
"May in God's name come inside!"

He who was out in the storm and rain
Drew back at the Geraldine's call.
"Now who comes not in the Holy Name
Will never come in at all."

He looked to the right, he looked to the left,
And never a one saw he;
But right in his path lay a coal black hound,
A-moaning right piteously.

"Come in," he cried, "you little black hound.
Come in, I will ease your pain;
My roof shall keep you to-night at least
From the leash of wind and rain."

The Geraldine took up the little black hound,
And put him down by the fire.
"So sleep you there, poor wandering one.
As long as your he^ desire."

The Geraldine tossed on his bed that night,
And never asleep went he
For the crowing of his httle red cock.
That did crow most woefully.

For the howling of his own wolf-hound.
That cried at the gate all night.
He rose and went to the banquet hall
At the first of morning light.

He looked to the right, he looked to the left.
At the rug which the dog lay on;
But the reindeer skin was burnt in two,
And the little black hound was gone.

And, traced in the ashes, these words he read:
"For the soul of your firstborn son,
I will make you rich as you once were rich
Ere the glass of your luck was run."

The Geraldine went to the west window,
And then he went to the east,
And saw his desolate pasture fields,
And the stables without a beast.

"So be it, as I love no woman,
No son shall ever be mine;
I would that my stables were full of steeds,
And my cellars were full of wine.

"I swear it, as I love no woman.
And never a son have I,
I would that my sheep and their little lambs
Should flourish and multiply.

"So yours be the soul of my firstborn son."
Here the Geraldine slily smiled,
But from the dark of the lonely room
Came the cry of a little child.

The Geraldine went to the west window,
He opened, and out did lean.

And lo! the pastures were full of kine,
All chewing the grass so green.

And quickly he went to the east window,
And his face was pale to see.
For lo! he saw to the empty stalls
Brave steeds go three by three.

The Geraldine went to the great hall door.
In wonder at what had been.
And up there came the prettiest maid
That ever his eyes had seen.

And long he looked at the pretty young maid,
And swore there was none so fair;
And his heart went out of him like a hound,
And hers like a timid hare.

Each day he followed her up and down.
And each night he could not rest.
Until at last the pretty young maid
Her love for him all confessed.

They wooed and they wed, and the days went by
As quick as such good days will,
And at last came the cry of his firstborn son
The cup of his joy to fill.

And the summer passed, and the winter came;
Right fair was the child to see.
And he laughed at the shriek of a bitter storm
As he sat on his father's knee.

Who rings so loud at the Geraldine's gate?
Who knocks so loud at the door?
"Now rise you up, my pretty young wife.
For twice they have knocked before."

Quickly she opened the great hall door,
And "Welcome you in," she cried,
But there only entered a little black hound,
And he would not be denied.

When the Geraldine saw the little black dog,
He rose with a fearful cry,
"I sold my child to the Devil's hound
In forgotten days gone by."

He drew his sword on the little black hound,
But it would not pierce its skin.
He tried to pray, but his lips were dumb
Because of his grievous sin.

Then the fair young wife took the black hound's throat
Both her small white hands between.
And he thought he saw one of God's angels
Where his sweet young wife had been.

Then he thought he saw from God's spirit
The hound go sore oppressed,
But he woke to find his own dead wife
With her dead child on her breast.

Quickly he went to the west window,
Quickly he went to the east;
No help in the desolate pasture fields,
Or the stables that held no beast.

He flung himself at his white wife's side,
And the dead lips moved and smiled,
Then came somewhere from the lonely room
The laugh of a little child.

THE LITTLE SISTER

The wind knocks at the window,
And my heart is full of fear.
For I know when it is calling
That some evil thing is near.

It whispers in the chimney,
And I strike the log to name,
Lest it come down and take me
To the land that hath no name.

For once I had a sister,
Who now am left alone,
And here we sat together,
When the wind did sigh and moan«.

There came a gentle knocking
Quick and sudden at the door.
And my sister hushed my terror.
Saying, "'Tis the wind, a-stór!"

She took my arms from round her,
She kissed me, cheek and chin,
But I cried, "Oh, little sister.
Do not let the robber in!"

She rose up from me laughing,
But her face was strange and white.
And she opened wide the window,
Looking long into the night.

And I said, "Oh, little sister,
There is on your cheek a tear!"
"'Tis but the rain," she whispered;
But my heart was full of fear.

And I said, "Oh, little sister.
There's a hand upon the door."
Soft she chid me from my crying,
Saying, "'Tis the wind, a-stór."

And turning from me smiling.
She took down the bar and chain,
But her cheek was like the lily
As she went into the rain.

And I said, "Oh, little sister,
Will you then return no more?"
But I only heard the pushing
Of the wind upon the door.

Long I cried, "Oh, little sister.
Will you soon come back again?"
But I only heard the beating
Of the storm upon the pane.

Now my mother sits in sorrow,
Weeping all the livelong day;
And I think she dreads the robber
Who did take her child away.

So I put up bar and shutter
When the wind goes howling by.
For I know when it comes knocking
That some evil thing is nigh.

THE LONE OF SOUL

The world has many lovers, but the one
She loves the best is he within whose heart
She but half-reigning queen and mistress is;
Whose lonely soul for ever stands apart,

Who from her face will ever turn away,
Who but half-hearing listens to her voice,
Whose heart beats to her passion, but whose soul
Within her presence never will rejoice.

What land has let the dreamer from its gates.
What face beloved hides from him away?
A dreamer outcast from some world of dreams,
He goes for ever lonely on his way.

The wedded body and the single soul.
Beside his mate he shall most mateless stand.
For ever to dream of that unseen face—
For ever to sigh for that enchanted land.

Like a great pine upon some Alpine height,
Tom by the winds and bent beneath the snow,
Half overthrown by icy avalanche.
The lone of soul throughout the world must go.

Alone among his kind he stands alone,
Tom by the passions of his own strange heart,
Stoned by continual wreckage of his dreams,
He in me crowd for ever is apart.

Like the great pine that, rocking no sweet nest,
Swings no young birds to sleep upon the bough.
But where the raven only comes to croak—
"There lives no man more desolate than thou!"

So goes the lone of soul amid the world—
No love upon his breast, with singing, cheers;
But Sorrow builds her home within his heart.
And, nesting there, will rear her brood of tears.

THE LOVER

He walks like one enchanted,
Whose soul is held in thrall,

By some sweet presence haunted
Who passed unseen by all.

He speaks as half-forgetting
The hearers that are by,
He sighs as though regretting
Some dear and soft reply.

It is a lover's rapture.
Naught doth he see or hear,
His heart is held in capture
Unto some mistress dear.

THE MAN WHO TROD ON SLEEPING GRASS

In a field by Cahirconlish
I stood on sleeping grass,
No cry I made to Heaven
Prom my dumb lips would pass.

Three days, three nights I slumbered,
And till I woke again
Those I have loved have sought me,
And sorrowed all in vain.

My neighbours still upbraid me,
And murmur as I pass,
"There goes a man enchanted.
He trod on fairy grass."

My little ones around me,
They claim my old caress,
I push them roughly from me
With hands that cannot bless.

My wife upon my shoulder
A bitter tear lets fall,
I turn away in anger
And love her not at all.

For like a man surrounded.
In some sun-haunted lane.
By countless wings that follow,
A grey and stinging chain,

Around my head for ever

I hear small voices speak
In tongues I cannot follow,
I know not what they seek.

I raise my hands to find them
When autumn winds go by,
And see between my fingers
A broken smnmer fly.

I raise my hands to hold them
When winter days are near,
And clasp a falling snowflake
That breaks into a tear.

And ever follows laughter
That echoes through my heart.
From some delights forgotten
Where once I had a part

What love comes, half-remembered.
In half-forgotten bliss?
Who lay upon my bosom,
And had no human kiss?

Where is the land I loved in?
What music did I sing
That left my ears enchanted
Inside the fairy ring?

I see my neighbours shudder,
And whisper as I pass:
"Three nights the fairies stole him;
He trod on sleeping grass."

THE LOVER'S ALMANAC

Oh, hearts that wear the willow,
To you I tell my woe,
Why thus uncared, ungartered,
And all so pale I go.

Come, you wan lovers sighing
Who too have felt the thorn.
But let none heart-whole linger
To laugh my grief to scorn.

Demure in church on Sunday
My love I chanced to see.
Amidst her gentle praying
I vow she looked on me.

On Monday in the meadow
I lingered by the stile,
She did but touch my fingers.
And passed me with a smile.

On Tuesday, mute and rosy,
I stood upon her way,
My heart it nigh betrayed me,
"Good-morrow," did she say.

With blushing cheek on Wednesday
Her path she went all slow;
How feared I such a fair maid?—
I could not move to go.

On Thursday, brave and daring,
I vowed I'd speak her fair,
She turned her glances from me,
And passed me, head in air.

All pale on Friday morning
I waited by her path,
She flashed her eyes upon me,
And pierced me with their wrath.

On Saturday, if that day
Should ever dawn for me,
I'll die for cruel Chloris
Beneath the cypress-tree.

THE MOTHER

"Ho!" said the child, "how fine the horses go,
With nodding plumes, with measured step and slow
Who rides within this coach, is he not great?
Some King, I think, for see, he rides in state!"

I turned, and saw a little coffin lie
Half-hid in flowers as the slow steeds went by.
So small a woman's arms might hold it pressed
As some rare jewel-casket to her breast;

Or like Pandora's box with pulsing lid
Where throbbing thoughts must lie for ever hid.
"Why this? why this?" comes forth the panting breath,
"And was I born to taste of nought save death?"

"Ho!" said the child, "how the proud horses shake
Their silver harness till they music make.
Who drives abroad with all this majesty?
Is it some Prince who fain his world would see?"

And as I looked I saw through the dim glass
Of one sad coach that all so slow did pass
A woman's face — 3. mother's eyes ablaze
Seize on the child in fierce and famished gaze.

"Death drives," I said, and drew him in alarm
Within the shelter of my circling arm.
So in my heart cried out a thousand fears,
"A King goes past." He wondered at my tears.

THE MOUNTAIN MAID

Half seated on a mossy crag,
Half crouching in the heather;
I found a little Irish maid,
All in June's golden weather.

Like some fond hand that loved the child,
The wind tossed back her tresses;
The heath-bells touched her unclad feet
With shy and soft caresses.

A mountain linnet flung his song
Into the air around her;
But all in vain the splendid hour,
For deep in woe I found her.

"Ahone! Ahone! Ahone!" she wept,
The tears fell fast and faster;
I sat myself beside her there,
To hear of her disaster.

Like dew on roses down her cheek
The diamond drops were stealing;
She laid her two brown hands in mine,

Her trouble all revealing.

Alas! Alas! the tale she told
In Gaelic low and tender;
A plague upon my Saxon tongue,
I could not comprehend her.

THE PHANTOM DEER

"Do you hunt alone to-day, O Red Richard!
Pray you tell me, do you hunt all your lone?"
"Ay, I am for the chase, Uttle cousin,
And wish no other spearing save my own."

"And whither are you going, O Red Richard!
That I may from the terrace watch your way?"
"All deep within the magic woods of Toonagh,
It is there that my hunting is to-day."

He vaulted to the saddle of his palfrey,
And laid across his arm the bridle-rein;
And he drew her to his knee, all fair and rosy.
Laughed—"A kiss, child, to bring me home again."

Then he rode on all so gay, so forgetting.
His light kiss as a flame upon her cheek;
But she went back alone into her chamber,
There to weep like her tender heart would break.

"O my love I though you love me not. Red Richard,
As you ride with your heart all whole and gay"—
She drew from her breast a magic potion.
Saying, "Sweet will your hunting be to-day."

"Three drops for you I drink, O Cousin Richard!
Three drops that you may have your heart's desire;
As a white deer I shall spring the glades before you.
Right merry shall you follow till you tire."

Now came upon the pathway of Red Richard,
As he rode through the arbours of the wood,
A white doe, so beautiful and trembling
That all disarmed and wondering he stood.

"Very sweet you are and fair," said Red Richard,
"Pretty doe, like a woman soft and white;

I could swear yours were the dark eyes of my cousin
That gaze with the sad mystery of night."

Then he laughed, and the deer, all quickly turning,
Sprang before him through the glades deep and green;
Hot, he followed with his spear ever ready—
Oh, such hunting as this was never seen!

He followed her all fast by stream and valley,
He followed her all dose through bog and briar;
Thrice she lured him round the woods by his castle.
But vanished ere he had his red desire.

And he rode home all slow and heavy-hearted,
And from his weary steed he flung him down;
There he saw on the terrace watching for him
A little maid all clad in snowy gown.

And he cried, "Come you hither, little cousin,
I swear that it was one as fair as you,
Clad in white, with her eyes as dark and splendid,
Who has fooled me so the glowing morning through.

"I promise to you, pretty," laughed Red Richard,
"To-morrow I shall bring her to your feet";
Then she said, smihng low, the Uttle cousin,
"Oh, to-morrow may your hunting be as sweet!"

When the dawn was pale and young came Red Richard
Through his castle gate into the magic wood;
And there upon his path, aloof and trembling,
The slender doe all palpitating stood.
And he chased her then by rock and by river.
He chased her long by meadow and by hill:
Thrice she took him through the gardens of his castle,
But she vanished ere his spear had had its will.

And so home, foiled and furious, rode Red Richard;
He flung himself all weary in his chair.
And beside him came the white little maiden,
Saying, "Cousin, was your hunting very fair?"

Then he laughed. "But to-morrow I shall win her,
Though she go where no foot has ever been.
To your feet will I bring her, pretty cousin;
Oh, such hunting as mine was never seen!"

Up at dawn, glad and eager, rose Red Richard;

The quickest steed in all the land had he,
And he rode to the magic woods of Toonagh—
There the white doe was grazing peacefully.

And then upon the tender moss behind her,
So softly and so swiftly did he ride,
Then she bounded but a pace from her resting
Ere his hot spear was red within her side.

And he tracked her through the mist and through shadow.
He followed the wet crimson on his way;
And he vowed he would have her dead or living.
Or follow her until the Judgment Day.

All red was the pathway to his castle.
And all eager and full fierce was his quest,
Till he came upon the corpse of his cousin—
With his sharp spear deep buried in her breast

So it is that the magic woods of Toonagh
Are haunted by the spirit of a deer:
She wanders by the castle of Red Richard—
Within her side the wounding of a spear.

THE ONE FORGOTTEN

A spirit speeding down on All Souls' Eve
From the wide gates of that mysterious shore
Where sleep the dead, sung softly and yet sweet
"So gay a wind was never heard before,"
The old man said, and listened by the fire;
And, "'Tis the souls that pass us on their way,"
The young maids whispered, clinging side by side.
So left their glowing nuts awhile to pray.

Still the pale spirit, singing through the night.
Came to this window, looking from the dark
Into the room; then passing to the door,
Where crouched the whining dog, afraid to bark,
Tapped gently without answer, pressed the latch.
Pushed softly open, and then tapped once more.
The maidens cried, when seeking for the ring,
"How strange a wind is blowing on the door!"

And said the old man, crouching to the fire:
"Draw close your chairs, for colder falls the night;

Push fast the door, and pull the curtains to,
For it is dreary in the moon's pale light"
And then his daughter's daughter with her hand
Passed over salt and clay to touch the ring,
Said low, "The old need fire, but ah! the young
Have that within their heart to flame and sting."

And then the spirit, moving from her place,
Touched there a shoulder, whispered m each ear,
Bent by the old man, nodding in his chair,
But no one heeded her, or seemed to hear.
Then crew the black cock, and so weeping sore
She went alone into the night again,
And said the greybeard, reaching for his glass,
"How sad a wind blows on the window-pane!"

And then from dreaming the long dreams of age
He woke, remembering, and let fall a tear:
"Alas! I have forgot—and have you gone?—
I set no chair to welcome you, my dear."
And said the maidens, laughing in their play,
"How he goes groaning, wrinkled-faced and hoar,
He is so old, and angry with his age—
Hush I hear the banshee sobbing past the door."

THE PRIEST'S BROTHER

Thrice in the night the priest arose
From broken sleep to kneel and pray.
"Hush, poor ghost, till the red cock crows,
And I a Mass for your soul may say."

Thrice he went to the chamber cold,
Where, stiff and still uncoffined,
His brother lay, his beads he told,
And "Rest, poor spirit, rest," he said.

Thrice lay the old priest down to sleep
Before the morning bell should toll;
But still he heard—and woke to weep—
The crying of his brother's soul.

All through the dark, till dawn was pale,
The priest tossed in his misery,
With muffled ears to hide the wail.
The voice of that ghost's agony.

At last the red cock flaps his wings
To trumpet of a day new-born.
The lark, awaking, soaring sings
Into the bosom of the morn.

The priest before the altar stands,
He hears the spirit call for peace;
He beats his breast with shaking hands.
"O Father, grant this soul's release.

"Most Just and Merciful, set free
From Purgatory's awful night
This sinner's soul, to fly to Thee,
And rest for ever in Thy sight."

The Mass is over—still the clerk
Kneels pallid in the morning glow.
He said, "From evils of the dark
Oh, bless me, father, ere you go.

"Benediction, that I may rest.
For all night did the banshee weep."
The priest raised up his hands and blest—
"Go now, my child, and you will sleep."

The priest went down the vestry stair,
He laid his vestments in their place,
And turned—a pale ghost met him there,
With beads of pain upon his face.

"Brother," he said, "you have gained me peace.
But why so long did you know my tears,
And say no Mass for my soul's release.
To save the torture of all those years?"

"God rest you, brother," the good priest said,
"No years have passed—but a single night."
He showed the body uncoffinèd.
And the six wax candles still alight.

The living flowers on the dead man's breast
Blew out a perfume sweet and strong.
The spirit paused ere he passed to rest—
"God save your soul from a night so long."

Who was stealing the Baron's wine,
Golden sherry and port so old,
Precious, I wot, as drops of gold?
Lone to-night he came to dine,

Flung himself in his oaken chair,
Kicked the hound that whined for bread;
"God ! the thief shall swing!" he said,
Thrust his hand through his ruffled hair.

Bolt and bar and double chain
Held secure the cellar door;
And the watchman placed before,
Kept a faithful watch in vain.

Every day the story came,
"Master, come! I hear it drip!"
The wine is wet on the robber's lip,
Who the robber, none could name.

All the folk in County Clare
Found a task for every day
By the Baron's gate to stray.
Came to gossip, stayed to stare.

Nothing here to satisfy
Souls for tragedy awake;
Just the castle by the lake.
Calmest spot beneath the sky.

But the whispered story grew,
When the Baron went to dine,
That a devil shared his wine,
Had his soul in danger too.

Every morn the Baron rose
More morose and full of age;
Passed the day in sullen rage,
Barred his gates on friends or foes.

Lone to-night he came to dine,
Struck the hound that asked a share,
Heard a step upon the stair—
"Come, the thief is at your wine!"

Baron of Killowen keep

Running down the vaulted way.
To the cellar dark by day,
Took the ten steps at a leap.

There he listened with the throng
Of frighted servants at the door,
He heard the wine drip on the floor.
And sea-mew's laughter loud and long.

Of oaken beam, of bolt and chain
They freed the door, and crowded through,
Their eyes a horror claimed in vain,
Nor ghost nor devil met their view.

They searched behind the hogshead, where
The watchful spider spied and span;
They sighed to see the wine that ran
A crimson torrent, wasting there.

They even searched the gloomy well
That legend said rose from the lake;
They saw bright bubbles rise and break,
But nothing stranger here befell.

The Baron swore—the Baron said,
"Now all be gone, alone I'll stay,
There shall not rise another day
Without this thief, alive or dead."

So still he stood, no sound was there.
But wasting wine fell drop and drip;
Save that, the silence seemed to slip
Its threatening fingers through his hair.

And then at last an echo flew,
The splash of waters thrown apart;
He cursed the beating of his heart
Because the thief was listening too.

The slipping scrape of scales he hears.
And sea-mew laughter, loud and sweet;
He dares not move his frightened feet.
His pulse beats with a thousand fears.

At that strange monster in the gloom
He points his pistol quick, and fires;
Before the powder spark expires
He hears a sea-bird's scream of doom.

He saw one gleam of foam-white arms.
Of sea-green eyes, of sloak brown hair;
He had a glance to find her fair.
When he had slain her thousand charms.

The Baron of Killowen slew
A strange sea-maiden, young and fair;
And all the folk in county Clare
Will tell you that the tale is true.

And when the Baron came to dine,
His guests could never understand.
That he should say, with glass in hand,
"I would the thief were at my wine!"

THE QUESTION

Now here is where I fail to understand,
And put my question in all reverence,
On bended Imee with head most lowly bent,
To the All-High, All-Knowing Providence.

A girl whose fate had left her widowed poor,
with three small babes to shelter and direct.
Rose to the burden, glad in her own strength,
Of those young minds to be sole architect:

Up with the lark and singing with his song,
Of hope and love, watched by her helpless brood,
Toiled in the night when sdl but she had slept.
And wore her soft hands rough to bring them food.

At each sweet morn she opened wide the door
All to the sun, so that a golden ray
Would pierce the gloom, and like a torch of flame
Light up the bed where her three treasures lay.

Soft would she say, "See God's bright angel come
To bless my babes and chase away the night":
Then would she bend, all hungry in her love.
To kiss each waking child with new delight.

Each tender body she would robe with pride
And awe unceasing at the beauties shown,
In dimpled limb and cheek and silken hair,

In all the loveliness she called her own.

Then with much laughter would she drive them forth
From her small room until her work was done;
Where she could watch from out the open door,
And smile upon them playing in the sun.

One golden morn as she drove forth her brood
Of pretty chicks to meet the coming day,
She pointed where a mother throstle clung
With three young birds upon a flow'ry spray.

And as she watched, from the blue air swept down
A hawk, who for a dreadful moment still
Swung in the air, as counting, one, two, three,
Which frightened fledgling he would pounce to kill,

Then struck. She heard the mother's scream of rage,
Who in her wild despair went flying high,
Then dropt again beside the cowering two
That still remained, with sad and piteous cry.

"So death might swoop," the woman said, "on mine."
She kissed each babe and there let fall a tear:
"My little ones, so tender and so weak."
Into her heart there came an endless fear.

Was Hugh too pale, was Una's cheek too red,
Was Kathleen languid in her pretty play?
"O Lord! O Father! keep my darlings safe,"
She held the baby in her arms to pray.

And as she bent her down all full of prayer,
Above the nest that held her pretty brood:
To fold them close with her great mother's love
And fill each little mouth that called for food,

Then did the Hawk a moment hover high
Above the house, and swooping strike to kill
No tender fledgling—ah! less easy spared,
The mother fell to whet his cruel bill.

And I who passed and found the nest destroyed,
And heard the hungry and affrighted cry
Of each poor babe, beneath Death's cunning blow,
Who struck the whole because the one did die:

"Wherefore this strange destruction having made,

This contradiction of all Nature's ways?"
I put my question to High Providence,
And sUent knelt in pity and amaze.

THE RAIN

This is the rhyme of the rain on the roof,
Tears, all tears, slow falling tears—
If this is the warp, then what is the woof?
Flesh that sorrows and flesh that fears.

Ah! poor humanity, weeping sore,
Guilt and sorrow, anger and shame.
Oh I who could peace on this earth restore?
Who shall punish and who shall blame?

Here where a God, loved much, was slain.
Since He hath failed, then who can win?
On the thirsting ground let them fall again,
Tears of sorrow and tears of sin.

THE TEMPEST

Come, teasing wind, we will fly,
Seek our heart's desire, you and I;
Fit comrade for me,
Thou breath of liberty,
I sigh for the freedom of your wings.
The sea will make us horses for our speed,
The fields will give the perfume of their seed,
In the woods a sweet rose blowing,
We will scatter it in going,
And bear the lark up sunward as he sings.

Go! we must part, you and I;
Not this my heart's desire, so goodbye!
Had I thought a moment's madness
Had wrought so dire a sadness,
My soul had never sorrowed for thy wings.
What have the tossing waves found for their play?
Have mercy, let the white face hide away!
In the fields a harvest dead,
In the woods life's promise fled.
And the lark is blown seaward as he sings.

Far better you were sleeping, O my soul.
Than that your coming forth a moment stole
From another's heart its rest.
Die you silent in my breast
And seek in death that answer life denied:
Lest a dying voice should curse instead of pray,
Lest a heart should shadow, blighted of its May,
Lest a soul glad of its night
Should be plunged in gloom of night.
Be in the World's seeing satisfied.

THE WANDERERS

Out from her doorway peeped the little maid
To gaze upon the world most full of glee.
Her eager eyes all bright and unafraid,
Her smooth cheek flushed with joy of things to be.

Nor did she stay because long shadows fleet
Did seek the sun for some too slow eclipse;
She shut the door behind her daring feet,
And hastened forth, a song upon her lips.

Deep in her heart a timid dream's unrest,
A chidden thought not all forbid to stay,
Of how, as from life's fruit she plucked the best,
A splendid knight would ride upon her way.

There was for her no danger in the shade,
No evil in the whisper of the wind,
Out from her home sped forth the little maid,
And closed the door her eager feet behind.

Did you not know her? Woman, pale of cheek.
Dim-eyed and weary, pray you stop and tell—
The years are long, the grave is far to seek.
Rest you a little—you who knew her well.

The splendid youth—was he but all a dream?
Came he not forth in armour's bright array,
Fore of the battle did his banner stream.
In eager hand uplifted for the fray?

There at his gate he stood, the little knight,
For any maid a champion bold and fair,

In benediction lay a shaft of light
Upon his golden helm of silken hair.

He looked into the world, nor feared the shade,
High were his hopes of battles yet to be;
With his brave eyes he sought them unafraid
And for his watchword hath he purity.

The victor's laurels and the poet's crown,
The singer's lute, the soldier's sword, all won,
All that the world could hold of high renown.
As there he stood a-dreaming in the sun.

Do you remember, elder, sad and grey,
Behind his feet youth's portals clashing fell?
Worn in life's battle, broken in the fray,
Have you forgotten?—yet you knew him well.

THE WATCHER IN THE WOOD

Deep in the wood's recesses cool
I see the fairy dancers glide,
In doth of gold, in gown of green,
My lord and lady side by side.

But who has hung from leaf to leaf,
From flower to flower, a silken twine—
A cloud of grey that holds the dew
In globes of dear enchanted wine?

Or stretches far from branch to branch.
From thorn to thorn, in diamond rain.
Who caught the cup of crystal pure
And hung so fair the shining chain?

'Tis death, the spider, in his net,
Who lures the dancers as they glide,
In cloth of gold, in gown of green,
My lord and lady side by side.

THE WHITE WITCH

Heaven help your home to-night,
M'Cormac, for I know

A white witch woman is your bride:
You married for your woe.

You thought her but a simple maid
That roamed the mountain-side;
She put the witches glance on you,
And so became your bride.

But I have watched her close and long
And know her all too well;
I never churned before her glance
But evil luck befell.

Last week the cow beneath my hand
Gave out no milk at all;
I turned, and saw the pale-haired girl
Lean laughing by the wall.

"A little sup," she cried, "for me;
The day is hot and dry."
"Begone!" I said, "you witch's child,"
She laughed a loud goodbye.

And when the butter in the churn
Will never rise, I see
Beside the door the white witch girl
Has got her eyes on me.

At dawn to-day I met her out
Upon the mountain-side,
And all her slender finger-tips
Were each a crimson dyed.

Now I had gone to seek a lamb
The darkness sent astray:
Sore for a lamb the dawning winds
And sharp-beaked birds of prey.

But when I saw the white witch maid
With blood upon her gown,
I said, "I'm poorer by a lamb;
The witch has dragged it down."

And, "Why is this, your hands so red
All in the early day?"
I seized her by the shoulder fair.
She pulled herself away.

"It is the raddle on my hands,
The raddle all so red.
For I have marked M'Cormac's sheep
And little lambs," she said.

"And what is this upon your mouth
And on your cheek so white?"
"Oh, it is but the berries' stain";
She trembled in her fright.

"I swear it is no berries' stain.
Nor raddle all so red";
I laid my hands about her throat.
She shook me off, and fled.

I had not gone to follow her
A step upon the way,
When came I to my own lost lamb,
That dead and bloody lay.

"Come back," I cried, "you witch's child,
Come bade and answer me";
But no maid on the mountain-side
Could ever my eyes see.

I looked into the glowing east,
I looked into the south,
But did not see the slim young witch,
With crimson on her mouth.

Now, though I looked both well and long,
And saw no woman there,
Out from the bushes by my side
There crept a snow-white hare.

With knife in hand I followed it
By ditch, by bog, by hill:
I said, "Your luck be in your feet.
For I shall do you ill."

I said, "Come, be you fox or hare.
Or be you mountain maid,
I'll cut the witch's heart from you,
For mischief you have made."

She laid her spells upon my path,
The brambles held and tore,
The pebbles slipped beneath my feet,

The briars wounded sore.

And then she vanished from my eyes
Beside M'Cormac's farm,
I ran to catch her in the house
And keep the man from harm.

She stood with him beside the fire,
And when she saw my knife.
She flung herself upon his breast
And prayed he'd save her life.

"The woman is a witch," I cried,
"So cast her off from you";
"She'll be my wife to-day," he said,
"Be careful what you do!"

"The woman is a witch," I said;
He laughed both loud and long:
She laid her arms about his neck,
Her laugh was like a song.

"The woman is a witch," he mocked,
And laughed both long and loud;
She bent her head upon his breast,
Her hair was like a cloud.

I said, "See blood upon her mouth
And on each finger-tip!"
He said, "I see a pretty maid,
A rose upon her lip."

He took her slender hand in his
To kiss the stain away—
Oh, well she cast her spell on him,
What could I do but pray?

"May Heaven guard your house to-night!"
I whisper as I go,
"For you have won a witch for bride.
And married for your woe."

THE WOMAN WHO WENT TO HELL

AN IRISH LEGEND

Young Dermod stood by his mother's side,
And he spake right stern and cold;
"Now, why do you weep and wail," he said,
"And joy from my bride withhold?

"And why do you keen and cry," said he,
"So loud on my marriage day?
The wedding guests they now eager wait,
All clad in their rich array.

"The priest is ready with book and stole,
And you do this grievous thing:
You keep me back from the altar rail—
My bride from her wedding ring."

His mother she rose, and she dried her tears,
She took him by his right hand—
"The cause," she said, "of my grief and pain
Too soon must you understand.

"Oh, one-and-twenty long years ago
I walked in your father's farm,
I broke a bough from a ripe peach-tree,
And carried it on my arm.

"My heart was light as a thistle-seed—
I had but been wed a year—
I dreamt of joy that would soon be mine—
A babe in my arms so dear.

"There came to me there a stranger man,
And these are the words he spake:
'The fruit you carry I fain would buy,
I pray you my gold to take.'

"The fruit I carried he then did buy—
You lying beneath my heart—
I tended to him the ripe peach-bough
He tore the gold branch apart.

"He whispered then in my frightened ear
The name of the Evil One,
'And this have I bought to-day,' he said—
The soul of your unborn son.

"'The fruit you carry, which I did buy,
Will ripen before I claim;
And when the bells for his wedding ring

Again you shall hear my name.'"

Now Dermod rose from his mother's side,
And all loud and long laughed he.
He bore her down to the wedding-guests,
All sorrowful still was she.

"Now, cry no more, sweet mother," he said,
"For you are a doleful sight
And who is there in the banquet-hall
Can claim my soul to-night?"

Then one rose up from the wedding throng.
But his face no man could see,
And he said, "Now bid your dear farewell,
For your soul belongs to me."

Young Dermod stood like a stricken man.
His mother she swooned away;
But his love ran quick to the stranger's side.
And to him she this did say:—

"If you will let his young soul go free,
I will serve you true and well,
For seven long years to be your slave
In the bitterest place of hell."

"Seven long years, if you be my slave,
I will let his soul go free."
The stranger drew her then by the hand,
And into the night went he.

Seven long years did she serve him true
By the blazing gates of hell,
And on every soul that entered in
The tears of her sorrow fell.

Seven long years did she keep the place,
To open the doors accurst,
And every soul that her tear-drops knew —
It would neither burn nor thirst.

And once she let in her father dear.
And once passed her brother through,
Once came a friend she had loved full well,
Oh, bitter it was to do!

On the last day of the seven long years

She stood by her master's knee —
"A boon, a boon for the work well done
I pray that you grant to me.

"A boon, a boon, that I carry forth
What treasure my strength can bring."
"That you may do," said the Evil One,
"And all for a little thing.

"All you can carry you may take forth
By serving me seven years more."
Bitter she wept for the world and love.
But took her sad place by the door.

Seven long years did she serve him well
Until the last day was done,
And all the souls that she had let in,
They clung to her one by one.

And all the souls that she had let through
They clung to her dress and hair,
Until the burden that she brought forth
Was heavy as she could bear.

The first who stopped her upon her way
Was an angel with sword aflame,
"The Lord has sent for your load," he said,
"St. Michael it is my name."

The woman drew back his gown of white,
And the cloven hoof did see.
"Oh, God, be with me to-night," she cried,
"For bitter my sorrows be.

"I will not give it to you," she wept,
Quick grasping her burden tight;
And all the souls that surrounded her
Clung closer in dire affright.

The next who stopped her upon her way
Was a maid all fair to see,
And "Sister, your load is great," she said,
"So give it, I pray, to me."

"The Virgin, I am, God sent me forth
That you to your love might go,"
The woman she saw the phantom's eyes
And paled at their fierce red glow:

"I will not give it to you," said she,
And wept full many a tear.
And all the souls that her burden made
Cried out in desperate fear.

The third who met her upon her way
Was a Man with face so fair:
She knelt her down at his wounded feet,
And she laid her burden there.

"Oh I will give it to You" she said,
And fell in a swoon so deep,
The flying souls and their cries of joy
Did not wake her from her sleep.

Seven long days did her slumber last,
And, oh, but her dream was sweet,
She thought she wandered in God's far land,
The bliss of her hopes complete!

And when she woke on the seventh day
To her love's home did she go.
And there she met neither man nor maid
Who ever her face did know.

And lo! she saw set a wedding feast,
And tall by her own love's side
There leaned a maiden, all young and fair,
Who never should be his bride.

"A drink, a drink, my little page boy,
A drink I do pray you bring."
She took the goblet up in her hand,
And dropped in her golden ring.

"He who would marry, my little page,
I pray he may drink with me,
'To the old true love he has forgot,'
And this must his toasting be."

When her false lover had got the cup
He drained it both deep and dry,
"To my dead love that I mourned so long,
I would that she now were nigh."

He took from the cup the golden ring,
And he turned it in his hand;

He said, "Whoever has sent this charm
I cannot her power withstand."

"Oh she is weary, and sad, and old,"
The little page boy replied;
But Dermod strode through the startled guests,
And stood by his own love's side.

He took her up in his two strong arms,
And "Have you come home?" he said,
"Twice seven long years I mourned you well
As silent among the dead."

He kissed her twice on her faded cheek,
And thrice on her snow-white hair.
"And this is my own true wife," he said
To the guests who gathered there.

"Oh she is withered and old," they cried,
"And her hair is pale as snow.
'Twere better you took the fair young girl,
And let the sad old love go."

"I will not marry the fair young girl.
No woman I wed but this,
The sweet white rose of her cheek," said he,
"Shall redden beneath my kiss.

"There is no beauty in all the land
That can with her face compare."
He led her up to the table head.
And set her beside him there.

THE WOLF AND THE LAMB

She had hair gold as her father's corn;
She tripped and sung,
Like to a little lamb new-born,
So gay, so young.

She gathered lone in the long day's shade,
So soft, so shy,
Ripe berries red, poor little maid—
And he came by.

He loved youth well, and her years were few.

Was he ever young?
A cold heart hid 'neath his eyes stone blue.
And a honeyed tongue.

He loved gold hair, and her tresses strayed
Like the pale sunrise,
And a gentle gaze, poor little maid—
She had sweet eyes.

He rode all lone with his horse and hound,
Now his hunting done.
With his chin on breast and his eyes on ground
In the setting sun.

She gathered there in the long day's shade
Ripe fruit all red.
And Ufe was good, poor little maid,
She sung and said.

But Fate in an evil mood let slip
A rolling stone
In the steed's swift way, and it ran to trip
The frightened roan.

She leaned from the bush, all sore afraid
At the tumult there,
Her dimpled face, poor little maid.
And shining hair.

He stayed to woo and his love to tell
For an idle day,
Opened the gates of Heaven—of Hell—
Then rode away.

With a smile and a jest for his time delayed,
He came to town—
In the lake's deep heart, poor little maid.
She laid her down.

And I, who heard the tale retold,
Still wondering wait
Will the man some time, a thousandfold.
Repent her fate?

But he laughs to-day with his sin unpaid.
And she sleeping lies—
So white, so still—poor little maid,
She had sweet eyes.

Go not to the hills of Erinn
When the night winds are about,
Put up your bar and shutter,
And so keep the danger out.

For the good-folk whirl within it,
And they pull you by the hand,
And they push you on the shoulder,
Till you move to their command.

And lo ! you have forgotten
What you have known of tears.
And you will not remember
That the world goes full of years;

A year there is a lifetime,
And a second but a day,
And an older world will meet you
Each morn you come away.

Your wife grows old with weeping,
And your children one by one
Grow grey with nights of watching.
Before your dance is done.

And it will chance some morning
You will come home no more;
Your wife sees but a withered leaf
In the wind about the door.

And your children will inherit
The unrest of the wind,
They shall seek some face elusive.
And some land they never find.

When the wind is loud, they sighing
Go with hearts unsatisfied,
For some joy beyond remembrance,
For some memory denied.

And all your children's children,
They cannot sleep or rest.
When the wind is out in Erinn

And the sun is in the West.

THE YOUTH BEWITCHED

My fair-haired boy is sore bewitched,
He goes all full of grieving;
The web of gloom upon his brow
Is sure of fairy weaving.

His cheery laugh I never hear,
His voice is rough and chiding;
Upon his path some evil thing
Does watch him from its hiding.

Ahone! Ahone! I bid him tell
If he has trod unknowing
Upon the fairy sleeping grass
Or cut the thorn a-growing.

He only turns his head away.
His words are bitter hearing;
But, ah! he cannot silence so
A mother's heart from fearing.

Last night I made a waxen shape
To bring the witch before me,
So she could take the sullen lad.
And my bright child restore me.

Nine pins I thrust within its side
To pierce her heart to dying,
And laid it on the glowing turf.
So listened for her crying.

Soon pressed a hand upon the latch,
I feared the evil fairy;
But when I raised my frightened eyes
'Twas none but Dwyer's Mary.

I told her of the boy bewitched,
She listened unbelieving;
And said she knew to-morrow's eve
Would free him of his grieving.

She turned her blushing face aside,
Her voice was low and cheering;

But, ah I she cannot silence so
A mother's heart from fearing.

TIME AND THE LADY

Haste, maiden, haste! the spray has come to budding,
The dawn creeps o'er the heavens gold and fair.
Come, see the bud ere breaking, the languid day awaking.
"A moment, Time, until I bind my hair."

Come, maiden, come I the bud has burst to blossom.
The sun has kissed the earth and found it sweet.
Come, lest you lose, adorning, the beauty of the morning.
"A moment, Time, a moment, till I eat"

Come, maiden, come! ripe fruits are on the branches,
The evening star is glowing in the blue;
The breeze's breath grows colder. Come ere the day is older!
"A moment till I sip—I'm then with you."

Quick, maiden, quick I Death's hand has stripped the leafing;
Night frees her clouding hair from bonds that keep.
Quick I lest you're lost for ever, in the gloom to find me never.
"A moment, Time, a moment, till I sleep."

TO-MORROW

She walks in a lonely garden
On the path her feet have made,
With high-heeled shoes, gold-buckled.
And gown of a flowered brocade;

The hair that falls on her shoulders,
Half-held with a ribbon tie,
Once glowed like the wheat in autumn.
Now grey as a winter sky.

Time on her brow with rough fingers
Writes record of smiles and tears;
Her mind, like a golden timepiece,
He stopped in the long past years.

At the foot of the lonely garden,
She comes to the trysting-place

She knew of old, there she lingers,
A blush on her withered face.

The children out on the common,
They climb to the garden wall.
And laugh, "He will come to-morrow!"
Who never will come at all.

And often over our sewing,
As I and my neighbour sit
We gossip over this story
That never had end to it,

"He is dead," I say, "that lover,
Who left her so long ago,"
My neighbour rests her needle
To answer, "He's false I know.

"For could it be he were sleeping.
With love that was such as this
He'd break through the gates of silence.
And hurry to meet her kiss."

Is she best worth tears or laughter,
This dame in her old brocade?
My neighbour says she is holy,
With her faith that will not fade.

The children out on the common,
They answer her dreary call.
And say, "He will come to-morrow!"
Who never will come at all.

TO MONA

When dainty Mona walks this way
My foolish heart will beat.
And leaves me, though I turn aside,
To lie beneath her feet.

It follows her all up and down
More faithfully, I wis,
Than that be-ribboned spaniel which
She honours with a kiss!

And when all chidden by her frown

My heart creeps back to me,
It holds my breast a prison-house
And would again be free.

YOUNG UNA

Upon the shore young Una lies,
A smile upon her mouth;
Soft breezes kiss her heavy hair,
Slow blowing from the south.

Within the cabin on the hill
Her mother doth complain:
"God bless the child! her feet are slow
To bear her home again."

Her mother's mother, grey and old,
She laughs beside the fire:
"Once I was hot as she, a-stór.
To gain my heart's desire."

And Una, smiling on the sea,
She speaks no word at all,
But watches with untiring eyes
The waves that break and fall.

Far in the East her father's ship
Lifts the blue waves to foam.
Her father's hand upon the helm
Now guides the vessel home.

And he hath safe a robe of silk,
All gold as Una's hair;
Strange jewels, too, from out the West,
To deck his child so fair.

But Una with unclosing eyes
Looks long towards the South;
The spray hangs diamonds on her hair,
A smile is on her mouth.

Now Una's lover in the wood,
The wood beside the shore.
He breathes his passion to the night
"Oh, love me, love, a-stór."

He kneels beside another maid,
She leans to hear him speak,
His arm is on her shoulder wlute,
Her kiss is on his cheek.

But Una, lone upon the shore,
Cares naught for what may be;
She smiles beneath the changing sky,
On shadow-haunted sea.

WHEN YOU ARE ON THE SEA

How can I laugh or dance as others do,
Or ply my rock or reel?
My heart will still return to dreams of you
Beside my spinning-wheel.

My little dog he cried out in the dark,
He would not whisht for me:
I took him to my side—why did he bark
When you were on the sea?

I fear the red cock—if he crow to-night—
I keep him close and warm,
'Twere ill with me, if he should wake in fright
And you out in the storm.

I dare not smile for fear my laugh would ring
Across your dying ears;
O, if you, drifting, drowned, should hear me sing
And think I had not tears!

I never thought the sea could wake such waves,
Nor that such winds could be;
I never wept when other eyes grew blind
For some one on the sea.

But now I fear and pray all things for you.
How many dangers be!
I set my wheel aside, what can I do
When you are on the sea?

Poetry Collections
Verses (1893)
The Fairy Changeling and Other Poems (1897)
The Collected Poems of Dora Sigerson Shorter (1907)
New Poems (1913)
The Sad Years (1918)
The Tricolour, Poems of the Irish Revolution (1922)

Novels
The Country-House Party (1905)
The Story and Song of Black Roderick (1906)
Through Wintry Terrors (1907)

Short Story collections
The Father Confessor, Stories of Death and Danger (1900)

www.ingramcontent.com/pod-product-compliance
Lightning Source LLC
Chambersburg PA
CBHW060050050426
42448CB00011B/2377

* 9 7 8 1 7 8 5 4 3 8 5 3 0 *